KUNG FU
FOR
GIRLS

**SELF-DEFENCE
FOR DIVAS**
Simon Harrison

First published in Great Britain in 2003

10 9 8 7 6 5 4 3 2 1

First published by
Ebury Press
Random House
20 Vauxhall Bridge Road, London SW1V 2SA

Random House Australia (Pty) Limited
20 Alfred Street, Milsons Point, Sydney
New South Wales 2061, Australia

Random House New Zealand Limited
18 Poland Road, Glenfield
Auckland 10, New Zealand

Random House South Africa (Pty) Limited
Endulini, 5A Jubilee Road
Parktown 2193, South Africa

The Random House Group Limited Reg. No. 954009

www.randomhouse.co.uk

A CIP catalogue record for this book
is available from the British Library.

Cover Design by Philip King
Text design and typesetting by Philip King
Artwork assistant Rowan Lowe

ISBN 0091891698

Papers used by Ebury Press are natural, recyclable
products made from wood grown in sustainable forests.

Printed in China by Midas

When attempting the exercises and/or advice given in this book, you should proceed with due care and caution. The exercises and suggestions are guidelines for the healthy individual, and if you have any medical condition or are unsure whether you should perform certain exercises please consult your doctor. The Publisher and Author cannot accept responsibility for illness, injury, damage or economic loss arising out of the use, or misuse, of the information and advice contained in this book.

Acknowledgements

Dedicated to Mum, Dad and the rest of the family.
Thanks to Philip King for knowing a good idea when he
sees one, very special thanks to the lovely Njong and
Yasmine, 3 is the magic number, cheers mad Dave.
Thanks to A.M.A. & Co.

Kung Fu for Girls can be your pocket bodyguard. Carry it around with you, and it will help you take care of yourself wherever you are.

In Kung Fu for Girls you will find simple and practical self-defence techniques. Practice them with friends before you go out in the evening. They can be fun – and if you do them properly they will keep you safe from harm.

Simplicity is vital to successful self-defence. Your motto from now on is 'Keep It Simple. Simple Is Effective.' The initial letters spell KISSIE so, to help commit your objectives to memory, you should be saying KISSIE KISSIE to yourself over and over.

Your personal attitude to yourself and your surroundings is your first and most important barrier against the street criminal. Self-defence is also about stopping trouble before it starts. Knowing a few simple moves will increase your confidence; you'd be surprised how many potential attackers may well detect this and end up looking for an easier target.

If you do find yourself confronted on the street, remember that a moving target is harder to hit. A helpful motto for this situation is Turn Around and Run Away or TA-RA for short. This is usually very effective but if running away isn't an option, use some of the techniques from this book. Be creative – whether it's your favourite kitten heels or a mobile phone, use them to full effect and walk away unharmed. The sense of satisfaction will be immense.

You never know, you might even get a taste for Kung fu. If so, I suggest you build on what you've learnt here by attending professional classes*.

So now, get ready to enter a whole new world of Kung Fu – for Girls...

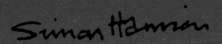

*For more information on martial arts go to www.bccma.com, the official governing body for Chinese Martial Arts in the UK.

BASICS

Imagine four women. They all look like you. One is casually dressed, confident. The second, a lost tourist. Next comes the nervous secretarial type in heels and a long coat. The last is also casually dressed but talking into a mobile. All of them are exhibiting the kind of subtle body language you interpret every day when making snap judgements about people's personalities.

Now imagine you are a misogynistic street crook. Which one of the 'yous' would you target first? List them in order of priority. There's no point complaining about this method of selection. You can't change the attitude of muggers, rapists and murderers by being outraged at their behaviour. You must change your own.

Know what makes you vulnerable to attack. Showing fear or being overtly nervous. Looking lost, wearing restrictive clothing, not paying attention and displaying expensive techno treats like minidisk players and mobiles are sometimes too much of a temptation for our crooked little friends.

On the street be prepared and be aware. Cultivate a preventive attitude.

The catchphrase for the street is 'be prepared and be aware'. Like it or not it's a hostile environment. If you are the sort of person who never worries about being attacked then you will probably never have a problem. But if you are anxious, here are a few tips.

Be aware of transitional phases. It takes the mind a few moments to adjust between one environment and another. This can apply to the transition from escalator to station exit. You are still digesting the information from the interior environment as you enter the exterior, which can make you vulnerable and careless. Before you leave the station take a look around. The same applies to the bus, restaurant, office or even your home. It is called anti-surveillance: a simple precaution that can put off a criminal because he sees you are aware and therefore not soft. You become a potential hazard – unpredictable and therefore a non-target.

Practice is essential. There is no substitute for practice and the perfection of movement you will accomplish from repetition of techniques with a partner. Except, maybe, dumb luck, which you simply can't rely on. The point of practice is to create what is called 'muscle memory'. When you learned to walk or to catch a ball, you created muscle memory. The idea with kung fu is to create muscle memory that is so efficient it bypasses the conventional avenues of physical behaviour, causing complex reactions to dangerous situations to be deeply embedded in your nervous system. Good kung fu is mindless. It's an expression of your body with minimum interference from the intellect. It's how animals react. Very primal.

How you stand is of fundamental importance. I am not talking about the flashy pose you strike. I'm referring to how strongly you are attached to the ground. Terms like 'steady', 'well grounded' and 'rooted' are appropriate here. The stronger your stance, the harder you will be able to hit your attacker. It's a simple hydraulic principle. If you are immovable and you hit someone, they move and you don't.

Here we have a left-handed and right-handed guard position. Study the front view carefully. It's arranged so that the hands can protect the face or body very quickly. They guard the centre line of your body. The knees are bent, balanced and ready to kick or spring in any direction. In combat you move on the balls of your feet. Flat-footed stances are stronger, but you need lots of practice to use them effectively.

This is just one of many guard positions.

Look into it. See what suits you.

This is your centre line. Attacking criminals are attracted to your centre line like insects to lamplight. They will direct their attacks almost exclusively at this region. With sex attackers, even their genitals are drawn here. They seek to undermine your balance and composure on every level. They attack your 'heart', the very core of your being.

If your centre line is an intimate dinner party for a few special friends, then the criminal street attacker is the gatecrasher from hell.

My job is to provide you with five highly motivated, scary bouncers to kick, jab, gouge, scratch, elbow, knee, bite and head-butt him right back out again, should he be obtuse enough to invade your privacy. Use your limbs to create a forbidding metaphorical wall of heavily muscled, bald-headed men with pitted, unsmiling faces.

Guard your centre line. And attack his. Always come back to your centre line if your arms aren't engaged in grabbing, blocking or attacking. It's a good habit to have.

Finally, don't just fall into a fighting stance at the drop of a hat. You'll ruin the surprise for him when you start to slap him silly and that wouldn't be fair. Maintain the element of surprise until the last possible instant.

Use any means at your disposal to win. Fight back and make him regret his decision to pick on you as a target. If your fighting is precise, measured and accurate, he will stand little chance. You will walk away unharmed and a little wiser. That's good enough for me.

This is the dangerous bloke. Great waves of greed and desire slosh about inside his head, overpowering all sense of reason and human dignity. He is a menace. But, as he hurtles towards you, he suffers two major disadvantages. By assuming you are weak and therefore an easy target, it increases your element of surprise, making it a cinch for you to deck him. Not only will he not be expecting you to fight back, but this klutz is oblivious to the fact that he is literally oozing weak points. Here are a few:

1. The ears. Bite or grab them. Use them to manipulate his head. Slap them hard to deafen him.

2. The eyes. Jab and gouge with your fingers. If he can't see you, he can't fight. Also, if you get the chance, spit in them.

3. The nose. Hit with open palm strikes to destroy vision by causing watery eyes, to break the delicate bones and to destroy balance. His head will automatically tip back when hit on the tip of the nose. Just shove him onto his back. Grab the nostrils – great for moving his head around.

4. The chin. Hit upwards from underneath with elbows, palms, knees or head butts. Catch him while he's talking and he will bite his own tongue off. Also good for manipulating balance.

5. The throat and neck. Strangle, gouge and hit. Nothing drops a man like a crushed larynx. Dig your fingers into the recess at the base of the throat between the collarbones.

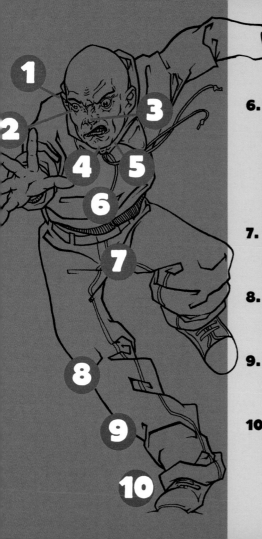

6. The body. For more advanced students, aim at the body. Targets are the sternum, collarbones, solar plexus, ribs and umbilical region. From behind, hit the spine, kidneys and nape of the neck.

7. The groin. Kick him in the gonads. Grab, knee or, god forbid, bite. All very effective.

8. The knees. Stomp on his knees with your feet to bend them back the wrong way.

9. The shins. Scrape them with the edge of your shoe. It takes the skin off.

10. The feet. Aim for the toes and the small delicate bones on the top of the foot.

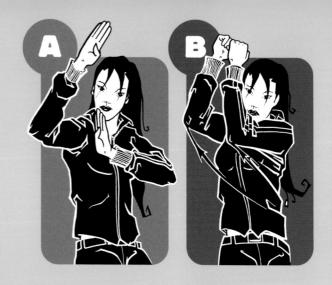

Blocks

Inside block to the side of the head

Assume the guard position. With your front arm, perform a military salute. Now move the saluting hand six inches forward, away from your head. Execute the movement again but go immediately to the finishing position illustrated. Any attack to the side of the head can be absorbed on the forearm. Your arm hacks into your attacker's like an axe hitting a tree branch.

Double-handed block

It serves the same purpose but is more heavily reinforced to absorb very powerful attacks. From the guard position, raise your hands to the side as if holding onto the dangling handle they have on tube trains. That's the blocking posture. Attacks are absorbed on the outside edge of the forearms.

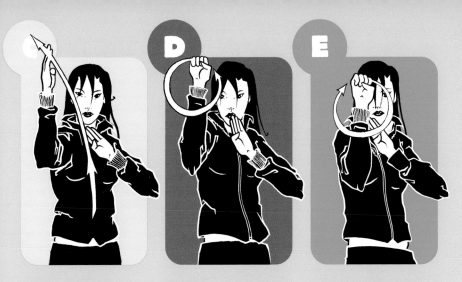

Lifting block

From the guard position, lift your forward arm and brush your hair back away from your forehead. Now imitate the same move again, but don't actually touch your head. This block will absorb an attack to the side of the head or a direct attack on the face if you catch it early enough.

Circling outer block

Hold up your hand in front of your face and imagine you are polishing a window. Circle your hand rapidly out away from your body and then back to the point of origin. Attack impact is absorbed on the outer forearm.

Circling inner block

Exactly the same principle as the previous move, but you reverse the circle and block with the inner forearm.

Low windscreen wiper block

From the guard position, sweep your arm down in a hacking arc like the inverted windscreen wiper of a car. This will block an attack to your body. Impact is absorbed on the outer forearm.

The slap block

Simply use the hook palm strike to drive your attacker's arm off to the side. Contact is made with the palm. Don't use the fingers – they'll get bent backwards and broken. Grabbing the sleeve of the aggressor makes it easier to control him.

1. The hands. Very versatile defence tools. Use fingertips to jab at the eyes and throat. Use nails to claw, gouge and rend facial skin and eyes. The outside edge of the hand can chop at the larynx and nose. The back of the hand can be slapped across the target's nose and mouth. The palm of the hand can be used to slap, thrust or push and the knuckles to punch, but try to avoid this as injuries are easy to incur.

2. The forearms. Use the inside and outside edges to slam your attacker in the head or neck.

3. The elbow. Deadly. Probably the hardest self-defence instrument on your upper body. It gets knocked about and leaned on so often that even the softest person has a conditioned, hard elbow. Use to scythe, jab and bludgeon.

4. The shoulder. Good for barging a man over when you have him off balance. Aim for the chest or abdomen.

5. The head. This is a tricky one because your head is a delicate area. The skull protects the brain so it's hard and can be used to butt the attacker's face – but if you're not used to the idea of doing this it can be quite a shock to the system. Be careful. It would be pointless to head-butt a man without the correct amount of conviction and knock yourself out. If you must butt, use your forehead. Try and avoid hitting him with your own face. That would be grotesque – I've seen it happen. If you're grabbed from behind, you can also use the back of your head – but, I say again, be careful.

6. From butts to butt. Yes, your arse is a weapon. It can be used to barge and strike, as you will learn later.

7. Knees. Very strong. Probably the strongest weapon on your lower body. Similar concept to the elbow. Knees have lots of leverage and make brilliant close-quarter weapons. Be careful not to hit with your kneecap, though. Use the area starting just above the kneecap to about a third of the way up your thigh.

8. The feet. They are tough, get stood on all day and are usually covered in shoes, so make use of them. Use the heel, the ball of the foot, the top of the foot, the toes if you are wearing rigid shoes, and the edges of the sole for scraping bones.

A

A lot of energy can be focused into your elbow. Leverage exerted from the waist is transmitted directly to the shoulder and loses little impetus before reaching the elbow. You actually hit with your waist, the arms transmit the power. This is called technical strength. And it's why a 9-stone woman can flatten a 13-stone man. To clarify your elbow position, imitate a chicken. Flap your stubby wings. Stop flapping and rotate at the waist.

Your elbows will create a slashing horizontal arc around your body. You simply swing and hit an attacker across the head, as illustrated.

The upward elbow strike is a vertical slashing motion of the elbow. Smell your armpit. Lift your arm and have a good sniff. Your arm should move approximately to the position illustrated. This attack connects with the underside of the chin. The free hand keeps his arm at bay.

Now grab his arm and drag it down. If the opportunity arises and you find yourself with a height advantage over your attacker, you can use the downward elbow strike. The technique begins at the upward elbow position. It descends rapidly into your attacker's exposed neck or back.

High kicks

High kicks look great on TV but in a desperate fight they can be slow and too elaborate. A kick to the head is harder to pull off effectively than a stomp to the knee. Remember, 'Keep It Simple, Simple Is Effective.'

23

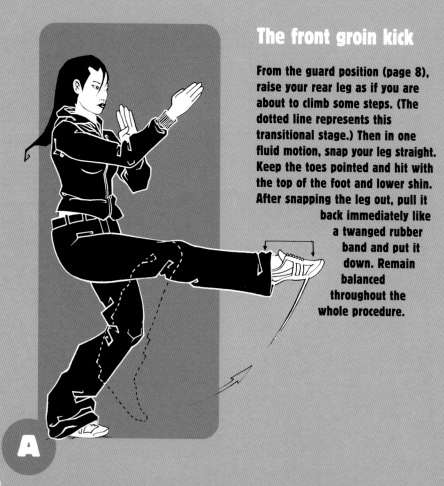

The front groin kick

From the guard position (page 8), raise your rear leg as if you are about to climb some steps. (The dotted line represents this transitional stage.) Then in one fluid motion, snap your leg straight. Keep the toes pointed and hit with the top of the foot and lower shin. After snapping the leg out, pull it back immediately like a twanged rubber band and put it down. Remain balanced throughout the whole procedure.

A

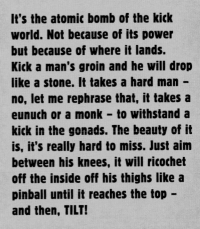

Groin kick in action

It's the atomic bomb of the kick world. Not because of its power but because of where it lands. Kick a man's groin and he will drop like a stone. It takes a hard man – no, let me rephrase that, it takes a eunuch or a monk – to withstand a kick in the gonads. The beauty of it is, it's really hard to miss. Just aim between his knees, it will ricochet off the inside off his thighs like a pinball until it reaches the top – and then, TILT!

Side stomp kick

This is a very powerful kick. Lift the leg as illustrated. Thrust down and strike with the heel. Avoid hitting with the toes. They can bend back and get injured. Your leg is in a direct line with your body so that your weight is behind the kick, focused at the heel. in this way, the technique holds a lot of power. Good long-range defence against a knife attack.

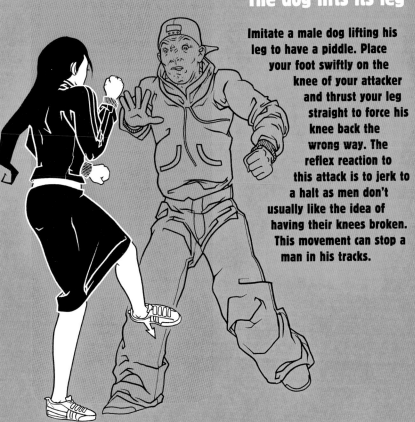

The dog lifts its leg

Imitate a male dog lifting his leg to have a piddle. Place your foot swiftly on the knee of your attacker and thrust your leg straight to force his knee back the wrong way. The reflex reaction to this attack is to jerk to a halt as men don't usually like the idea of having their knees broken. This movement can stop a man in his tracks.

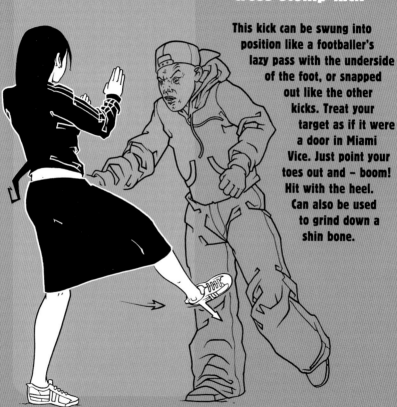

Cross stomp kick

This kick can be swung into position like a footballer's lazy pass with the underside of the foot, or snapped out like the other kicks. Treat your target as if it were a door in Miami Vice. Just point your toes out and – boom! Hit with the heel. Can also be used to grind down a shin bone.

Give him the boot

A knee strike on the groin is a man's nightmare, but other body targets are also effective. Here, the attacker is pulled onto the blow, which doubles in power as it rises up to meet his falling body. Lift leg high as if climbing steep steps. A fast, simple, close-quarter movement.

Give him five

You've all seen lengthy fist-fights on TV. No one gets cut, knuckles don't even bleed. To know what it really feels like to punch someone's skull, then try this quick test. Approach your bedroom door and punch it as hard as you can. Knuckles need to be properly aligned with forearm bones, so your wrist position must be correct. If it isn't, you will sprain your wrist when you hit your target because energy will dissipate into the wrist joint instead of up the forearm. Don't risk injury punching people in fights – use palm strikes instead.

Give him five

Palm striking is easy. From the guard position (page 8), thrust forward with either hand. Stretch back the fingers so the palm heel is exposed. This lowers the minimal risk of injury even further. You can curl your fingers, as illustrated, if you prefer. It makes little difference to power but some find it more comfortable.

Give him five

Assume the guard position (page 8) and then imagine you're holding a big beach ball directly in front of your face. The fingers point straight up. Pull one hand back and rotate your hips. The extended arm will form a slashing arc in front of your body, with the palm heel being the focus for power. Thrust with hips and arm. Bash him on the jaw or ear.

Weapons in your handbag

1. The mobile phone.
For use, see page 77.

2. Keys.
Grip them protruding from the bottom of your fist or arrange them so they protrude through the gaps between your knuckles to form a spiky fist. Use to jab, scratch and gouge.

3. Combs.
Use the same way as mobiles and keys.

4. Lipsticks, mascara.
Any longish, tough, plastic-packed accessory can be used to stab at your attacker's eyes and throat.

5. Hairspray.
Now I'm not sure of the legal implications of blinding a would-be rapist with your hairspray. I've even heard that, ludicrously, it may be classed as a firearm if used in this way. So obviously I wouldn't tell you to say, spray this substance into the eyes, nose or ears of your attacker or that if coupled with a lighter it makes a kick ass flame thrower. Because that would be irresponsible. Also, I'm not entirely sure how stable the lighter/ hairspray configuration is – SO, DEFINITELY DON'T TRY THIS AT HOME, OK?

6. A handful of change.
Hurl into the face of an attacker with a knife. This will give you time to escape. One-pound coins are the best, having a good size to weight ratio. But this can get expensive, so try not to meet too many rapists, muggers or murderers on one journey!

7. The handbag.
It can be used as a shield. The edges can be used to scuff at your attacker's face. You can use it to slap at his hands if he holds a weapon.

High heels look great but let's face it, they seem difficult to walk in comfortably and nearly impossible to run in with any degree of reasonable safety. But if you do have to fight in them, you might as well learn how to do it effectively. The heel can be used to stab at the attacker's feet, shins, knees, thigh muscles, groin, stomach and ribs.

The point of the heel inflicts horrible pain because all the power of your kick is focused behind that little point. If your attacker is knocked down, use the heel to stomp on him so that he

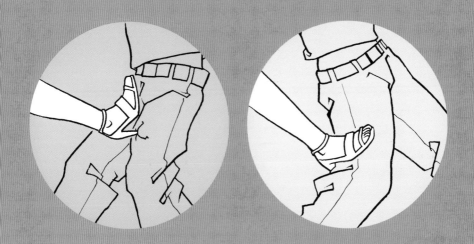

can't get up and chase you when you run away. Go for the ankles and knees, or his hands.

The inverted 'V' of the heel, the empty area between the heel and the flat portion of the sole that comes into contact with the floor, is great for trapping limbs. It gives good purchase on the backs of knees, as illustrated, and demonstrated later in the Stomp Kick Sneak Attack. Simply turn the foot to the side using a side stomp or a cross stomp kick to pin the limb from behind. Also, it's great to grind down the front of the shin bone.

If you are ever forced into a situation where you have to run for your life while wearing inappropriate footwear, try to take your shoes off. You must use your common sense here: you can't expect an attacker to pause while you fiddle with your shoe straps. Evaluate the situation and act accordingly. If you do get the high heels off, don't throw them away. Hold them as shown and use them like ice picks to climb the craggy body and pitted face of any mugger stupid enough to stand in your way. Pay particular attention to the bony areas of the head and face. Shoes used like this can cause shocking pain and if you hit him hard in the head they can penetrate the bone.

He will drop like he's been shot through the brain, so be careful when you use them.

If you can't get your shoes off, then use your keys. Just as effective. Hold as shown. Stab downwards at the head, neck and body or punch at the same targets.

The following pages are designed for you to see how techniques can be strung together to create combinations that flow in a logical sequence. Each move is dependent on your attacker's actions and his reactions to yours. The idea is to use your orientation and natural momentum to maximise the power of your counter-attacks and to manipulate your opponent so he is kept physically and psychologically off balance. This minimises the chance of him hitting you again once you have blocked his initial attack. These are highly confrontational counter-attacks, based on the assumption that you do not, as yet, have the necessary experience to step strategically. This is very hard to do properly and very easy to forget under pressure. Some strategic footwork manoeuvres are included at the end of the section and they are repeated later. If you can master the procedure and then remember to use it when someone is trying to throttle you, you will be practically street-invincible. For the meantime, here is how to deal with someone who is completely in your face.

TECHNIQUES

Block...

A

The attacker swings a big drunken punch at the side of your head. Use a lifting, outer circling or double-handed block to dissipate the blow. You must counter-attack immediately.

B

Grab his arm with the blocking hand and pull down to drag him off balance, then mash him across the jaw with a forward horizontal elbow strike. Watch out for flying tooth shrapnel.

C

Let go of his arm and hit him with a hook palm strike on the face. He will be falling into the blow, so you may need to dance out the way a bit and change your footing. Be prepared. Shout 'TIMBER!' as he hits the deck.

Block...

A

This time, as a preliminary to putting you in a head-lock, he reaches out to engulf your head with both arms. Work your arms between his and push his elbows out.

... give him the finger...

B

As soon as you get the opportunity, spread your fingers like a fan and dig them straight into his eyes. The bear-hug is now obstructed by your arms, which are attacking him while simultaneously defending you. His head will tip back as you hit his eyes.

... give him five.

C

As he tips his head back, smite him mightily on the chin. Use an open palm strike to destroy what little balance he has left and knock him flat on his back. Now would be a good time to follow up with a groin kick.

Block...

A

Block a direct punch to the face – or a grab for the throat – using lifting or outer-circling blocks.

B

Pivot your whole body while simultaneously assuming the chicken wing strike posture, and slam the point of your elbow straight onto his nose. Major downer for him. He will feel as if you stuck a 240 volt cable up his nostrils.

... give him the boot

C

Rotate back the opposite way and catch him on the rebound. Grab the back of his neck or head and drag him down for a knee strike to the body, neck or face. If you jerk his neck down fast enough, you can give him whiplash to add to his troubles.

Side step forty-five...

A

Step towards your attacker at 45 degrees. Cut across him as he lunges, making him overshoot and leaving his flank exposed. Keep your left arm and leg forward to block a right-handed attack. As he lunges for your throat or face, step forward and sideways by scooting your left leg diagonally across his direction of movement.

B

Smack his arm aside using the slap block with your left arm. Hit him just above the elbow. If he is wearing a jacket, grab the sleeve. He'll be deflected by your block, exposing his flank to you.

Drop your right arm onto his and use the combined force of both your arms to drive him further off course. This negates the danger of him retaliating with his other fist. It's too awkward for him to reach across his body. Lift your right leg. Bring the knee up high.

... stomp.

Side stomp the back of his knee. Drive his leg to the floor. You now have control over his upper and lower body. Pull him further off balance and elbow him in the face with the right arm. If you can master these steps you will be very difficult to beat.

53

A

B

This man is so angry he seems to want to eat your whole head. He's going for you with both hands. Step in towards him, reach between his arms and grab his ears hard.

Use his head like a steering wheel and make a sharp right or left turn. His head will tip in whichever direction you steer it because he wants to keep it attached to his ears.

Control his head and you control his balance. Steer him over sideways and kick him in the balls. Let go of his ears when he is thoroughly off balance. Finish him off with a knee strike. If you throw him slightly backwards, a kick will work just as well.

He will drop to the floor enveloped in great suffocating waves of pain and self-pity. If the situation is now under control you can walk away. If not, stamp on his ankle or knee while he is down, so he can't chase you if he gets up.

You're sitting on a bus, train or a park bench. Suddenly, a guy has his arm wrapped round your neck. He tries to drag you away by putting you in a neck lock. He will squeeze hard, but the following counter-attack works, even when the lock is on tight. It's also effective standing up.

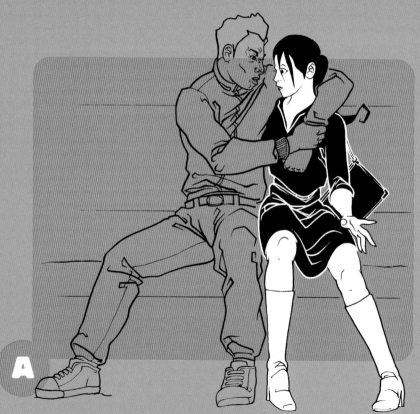

A

He's trying to choke you. Reach over his arm as shown. Then chop your arm up into his throat or chin. His head will tip back. Slide your hand up over his face and, for a truly efficient non-slip grip, get your fingers in his eyes and nostrils. Keep his head back at all costs.

B

It's now time for your second incapacitating technique of the evening. Punch the panther in his pants. Ignore the garbled pleas for mercy, they are obviously insincere, and hit him again. A couple of good whacks in the groin are enough to soften any man's resolve. Keep his head back.

Stand up and hit him in the throat with a 'Y' hand strike. Use the web of skin between your fingers and outstretched thumb to hit his throat or septum. If you hit him repeatedly in the throat he could die, so use your discretion. Now find another seat to sit on. This one will be quite a mess.

You dozed off on the train. When you wake up, a scary man in a nylon shell suit, white leather loafers and no socks is sticking his hand up your skirt. Typically, the carriage is empty apart from one man who suddenly gets interested in his newspaper. You will get no help from him.

A

60

Grab the assailant's wrist and place your other hand on his shoulder blade. You can hook your leg around his to increase the amount of control you will have over him later, but the technique works without it. Act fast because he'll be offended that you didn't like him feeling you up.

B

Pull his wrist up and stretch his arm away in the direction of the arrow. Then lever his shoulder forward and down so that it rotates in the joint and locks. If you've used your leg to trap him, he will possibly have a hyper extended knee at this point.

Stand up. Keep pulling and pushing in the direction of the arrows. Make sure you are balanced, then drop kick his head. Aim for the nose or put your toe in his eye. Then drop him and leave. Try not to start a fight with the chickenshit guy holding the newspaper.

You are grabbed from behind. Suddenly, there is a man trying to drag you away. If he puts his hand over your mouth to stop you screaming, bite his fingers. Repeatedly stomp on his foot till you get the desired reaction. Grind your heel down his shin. Then slam your elbow into his ribs.

B

C

This next move is quite a revelation. Ladies – your butt is a weapon! Lift your arms in a rapid arc to snap his grip and slam your buttocks backwards into his gonads. He will double over and lose balance. This technique looks a bit like a silly 60s dance move, but it works.

Stick your arms out like chicken wings and spin round to deliver a reverse elbow strike to the head or neck. If you've bumped him back out of range, move in quickly to finish him off with a kick to the knee or groin. Just pick your targets until he's dealt with.

A

Strangulation is one of the most common causes of death or injury during attacks on women, so learn to defend against it. Drop your chin until it touches the notch between your collarbones. This hides the weakest part of your throat and prevents immediate asphyxiation. Grab his elbows. Lift them from below by pushing up on them like a weightlifter. It throws him off balance and takes pressure off your neck. Kick him straight in the groin. You could also work your arms between his and stick your thumbs in his eyes. Or you could lift your arm as indicated and pull back the opposite leg.

Sweep your arm down in a hacking arc, using the low windscreen wiper block to effectively break the stranglehold and trap his arms. Squish them against your body with your blocking arm. You could now reverse elbow strike him with your left arm. Just follow the arrow.

B

Execute a palm strike to the underside of the nose or chin to drive his head back and destroy his balance. You could also gouge his eyes.

If he's still in range, grab both his shoulders and yank him forward for a knee strike to the groin. Pull him hard. The whiplash will disorient him. If he's further away, kick him. Either way, he will fall like a dead tree.

D

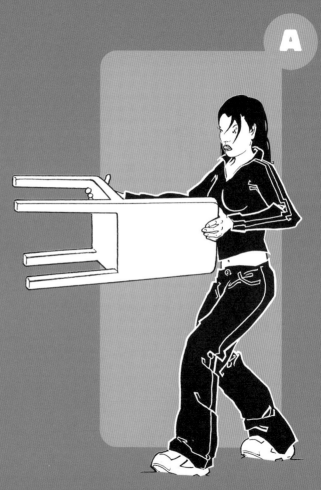

A

Contrary to popular belief, you do not swing chairs in a fight. It's way too slow and if the chair breaks you will be deprived of a useful weapon. It makes much more sense to grip the chair as illustrated and jab at your opponent with the legs. Furthermore, by rotating your hands in a steering wheel motion similar to that described in 'The Getaway' you add a whole new dimension to your line of defence.

In the way shown here, the chair becomes an effective deterrent and can be used to fend off even the most savage and determined assailants. Why do you think it's so popular with lion-tamers?

B

You know those awkward little tables that four of you try to squeeze round for your after-work drink? They're supported by a single trunk that splays out to form feet. They look great but are completely unstable if leaned on. Well, I have finally found a use for this foolish item of furniture. Should a situation deteriorate beyond the point of no return and you need to make a speedy escape, or help a friend, tip over the nearest table, pick it up by the stem or legs and deploy it before you like the shield of Spartacus. Use it to deflect hurled bottles, chairs, glasses and aggressive customers.

Long banqueting tables are common in pubs nowadays and they will probably have bench seating. Either of these can be utilised as a WMD (weapon of mass destruction). You will find them a bit on the heavy side, so why not share the load with a friend? With girls on either end you will sweep the crowd aside. Remember, be determined and maintain a steady course for the nearest exit. Long tables and benches act like the squeegees used by those annoying guys who try to clean your car windscreen at traffic lights, except the grey scummy residue you're left with at the end is made of people not soap. Both chair and table techniques are extremely effective defences should you ever have to fight off an intruder in your own home.

A

Barry Big Chips: the man with mental halitosis. He has no self-restraint or shame. The drunker he is, the worse he gets. As you stand at the bar minding your own business, Barry sidles up and drapes his arm round your shoulders. He mumbles something dull and inconsequential in your ear. Then he oversteps the line and grabs your boob.

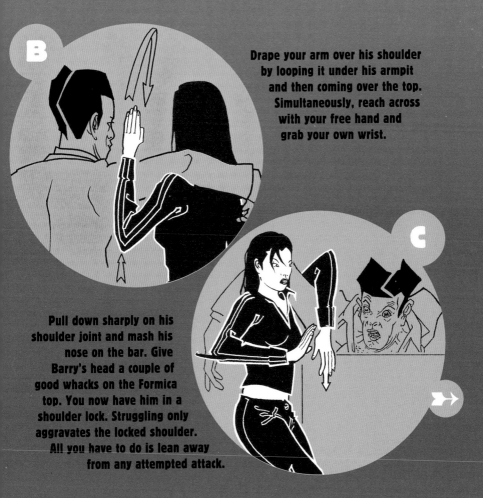

B

Drape your arm over his shoulder by looping it under his armpit and then coming over the top. Simultaneously, reach across with your free hand and grab your own wrist.

C

Pull down sharply on his shoulder joint and mash his nose on the bar. Give Barry's head a couple of good whacks on the Formica top. You now have him in a shoulder lock. Struggling only aggravates the locked shoulder. All you have to do is lean away from any attempted attack.

If properly executed, this technique is so quick that there is hardly time for his booze-addled brain to figure out how he got himself into such a ludicrous predicament.

FINISHING OPTIONS:

1. Drown him in his own beer (sadly illegal).
2. Call security and have the bounder ejected from the premises.

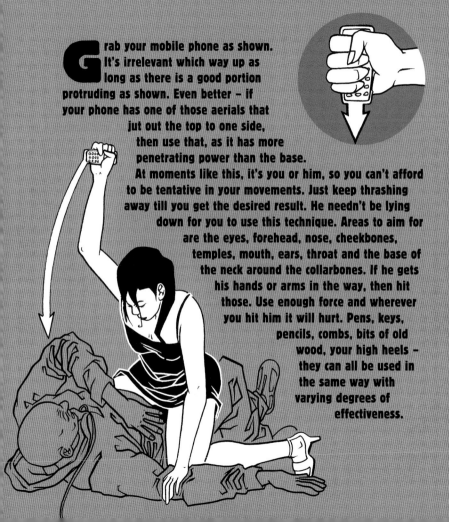

Grab your mobile phone as shown. It's irrelevant which way up as long as there is a good portion protruding as shown. Even better – if your phone has one of those aerials that jut out the top to one side, then use that, as it has more penetrating power than the base.

At moments like this, it's you or him, so you can't afford to be tentative in your movements. Just keep thrashing away till you get the desired result. He needn't be lying down for you to use this technique. Areas to aim for are the eyes, forehead, nose, cheekbones, temples, mouth, ears, throat and the base of the neck around the collarbones. If he gets his hands or arms in the way, then hit those. Use enough force and wherever you hit him it will hurt. Pens, keys, pencils, combs, bits of old wood, your high heels – they can all be used in the same way with varying degrees of effectiveness.

This is the only anti-knife technique where you're guaranteed not to get slashed or stabbed to death. I call it TA-RA.

It stands for Turn Around and Run Away.

Avoid a fight at all costs. Turn tail. There is nothing wrong with being terrified. Use the fear constructively to run like the clappers. Scream and shout. Make it plain to the whole street you don't want him near you. Sometimes this is enough to scare him off. Throw things at him to create opportunities for escape. Use anything to hand. Be creative, and always aim at his face. Try to temporarily blind him while you leg it out of there.

Pieces of clothing wrapped round your arm are good as shields. So are dustbin lids or even the whole dustbin. You can keep him at bay with your feet. Use the kicks described earlier to attack him from the waist down. In the end even a trained martial artist is wary of a knife, so if you want to learn how to deal with this situation, don't learn it from a book. Go to classes.

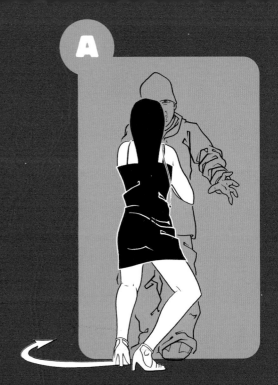

A

You are confronted by a knife attacker and will use a key fist as defence. As with the forty five and in manoeuvre, you will be stepping in towards your attacker at a 45 degree angle. You will cut across him as he lunges, making him overshoot the mark and leaving his flank exposed for attack. The girl in the image has her left arm and left leg forward and is blocking a right-handed attack. As the man lunges for your throat, chest or face, step forward and to the side by scooting your left leg diagonally across his direction of movement.

Smack his arm aside using the slap block with your left arm. Aim to hit him just above the elbow. If he's wearing a jacket, grab the sleeve and shove his arm aside. This forces his arm across his body, spinning him round and exposing his flank.

When you've pushed his arm down, across and out of the way, gouge his face open with your keys. This is no time for squeamish sensibilities. Either you repeatedly gouge him until he drops from shock, or he will kill you.

This move garrottes the attacker's neck. Begin the manoeuvre in the same position as the anti-knife technique. We are watching from the attacker's left hand side, so you can see the defender's arms. Use the same side step and slap block to avoid his attack. Then place your other leg behind his in order to trip him. Notice that the rear hand is lifted high.

B

We are now observing from the rear to give a clear image of the action, showing where you place your tripping leg and how the arm slices down. Shove his arm aside with your blocking hand and chop down with the free hand.

C

Back to the original left-hand view. His arm will drop when struck. Slide your arm straight up and clothes-line him in the neck with your forearm. If he gags and sticks his tongue out, hit his chin. He will bite his own tongue off. Hook backwards with a small leg movement to enhance his fall.

This move can be useful in a number of ways. You are grabbed by the throat, lose your balance and fall to the floor, or you are already on the floor and the man is trying to get on top of you and pin you down.

Drop your chin until it touches the notch between your collarbones. Push your arms between his and grab his head with both hands. Dig your nails in, work your thumbs into his eyes and drag his head forward to bite his nose. Plant your foot on his thigh. Stomp backwards. His leg will be forced back straight out behind him and he will lose his balance.

When he lands, he won't be able to see you because you had your thumbs in his eyes and chewed his nose off. If this didn't discourage him and he still looks active, stomp on his crown jewels with your stiletto heel. Get up and run.

Steer his head sideways, away from the kicking leg. In this case, the right arm rotates up and the left arm down, twisting his neck at an unbearable angle. He will go with it because you have your thumbs in his eyes. Jerk your shoulders off the floor in the direction of the head twist. Thrust him in the direction he is falling with your kicking leg and push him off.

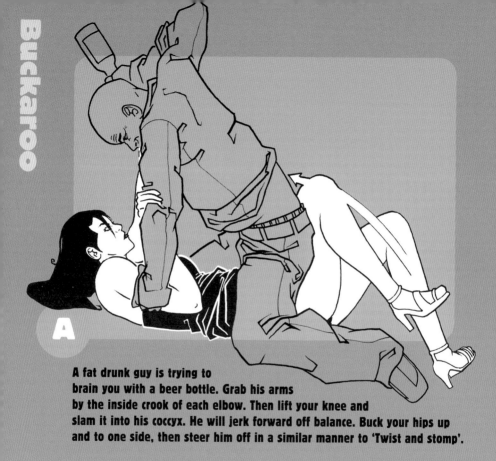

A

A fat drunk guy is trying to
brain you with a beer bottle. Grab his arms
by the inside crook of each elbow. Then lift your knee and
slam it into his coccyx. He will jerk forward off balance. Buck your hips up
and to one side, then steer him off in a similar manner to 'Twist and stomp'.

B

Steer him in the same direction you bucked him in. Lift
your shoulders off the ground and roll him away to the side.
Finish him with the stiletto stomp kick used in 'Twist and Stomp'.
Aim for something soft (not his head). Keep stomping till he looks
queasy, then get up and run away.

...ou rush to your friend's aid. A man is holding her down, strangling her, banging her head on the floor, or trying to snog her. Whatever, she doesn't want him there.

Reach over his head and grab his face. It's important to get a point of reference in a struggle like this, there's always a lot of movement, confusion and noise.

Go for the lips, nostrils and eyes. Claw his head backwards and administer a damn good spanking to the ear. Cup the striking hand as if using it to hold water. This creates a hollow palm which, when slammed over the ear, creates a seal and fills the brute's head with thunderous noise and blinding light. Keep hitting him until he falls off. Get your friend up and run.

Stomp kick sneak attack

You're out with your friends when a fight erupts. A man grabs your friend from behind and starts to choke or drag her away. Run up behind him and grab his shoulders, then stamp on the back of his knee. Use the side stomp or the cross stomp kick. Pull back and down with both arms and thrust your foot towards the ground at the angle indicated.

He will tip backwards. Reach round and grab his throat. Drag him further off balance until he is falling over. Pull him down far enough to get him in range of your finishing move. In this case, a downward elbow strike. Jump clear as he hits the deck. Your friend will be eternally grateful. Now would be a good time to ask her for any money she owes you.

At the end of the day, you are a nice, civilised person being confronted by someone who is not. Ultimately I want you to walk away from any attack safe and sound. But if you have to defend yourself, then you can scream, shout, kick, scratch, bite and spit. Vomit on him, for all I care. Fight back and make him regret his decision to pick on you as a target. If your fighting is precise, measured and accurate, he will stand little chance. You will walk away unharmed and a little wiser. That's good enough for me.

Simon